GREAT
SCIENTIFIC
THEORIES

Electricity

Richard and Louise Spilsbury

capstone

Published by Raintree, a Capstone Imprint
1710 Roe Crest Drive, North Mankato, Minnesota 56003.
www.mycapstone.com

Library of Congress Cataloging-in-Publication Data
Library of Congress Cataloging-in-Publication data is available on the Library of Congress website.

ISBN 978-1-4109-8727-3 (library hardcover) — 978-1-4109-8731-0 (paperback) —
ISBN 978-1-4109-8735-8 (eBook PDF)

Summary:
This book looks at the historical controversies that surround the discovery and theories of electricity and tells the stories of the scientists who worked on them. It also examines how the different theories based on electricity were arrived at, how they were tested, and what impact these theories and discoveries have had on our understanding of science today.

This book has been officially leveled by using the F&P Text Level Gradient™ System.

Editorial Credits
Helen Cox Cannons, editor; Terri Poburka, designer; Morgan Walters and Tracey Engel, media researchers; Steve Walker, production specialist

We would like to thank Dr. Rohini Giles at NASA's Jet Propulsion Laboratory for her invaluable help in the preparation of this book.

Photo Credits
We would like to thank the following for permission to reproduce photographs: Alamy Stock Photo: Lebrecht Music and Arts Photo Library, 25; Bridgeman Images: © Look and Learn/Private Collection/Kenneth John Petts, 7, © Look and Learn/Private Collection/Ron Embleton, 13, 21, 23, 29, Peter Newark Historical Pictures/Private Collection/Arthur David McCormick, 9; Capstone: Roger Stewart, 19; Getty Images Inc: Bettmann, 17; iStockphoto: JohnGollop, cover (map top, bottom); Paul Daly, 27; Rick Reeves: rickreevesstudio.com, 5, 11; Shutterstock: Andrey Armyagov, cover (middle), Andrey_Kuzmin, 2-3 background, Antony McAulay, 26, grafvision, cover (right), ilolab, vintage paper texture, Melkor3D, 15, Molodec, maps, Nik Merkulov, grunge background, pingebat, pirate icons, sharpner, map directions to island treasure, Triff, nautical background, TyBy, cover (banner)

TABLE OF CONTENTS

Some words are shown in bold, **like this**.
You can find out what they mean by
looking in the glossary.

TESTING THEORIES

For hundreds of years, scientists have tried to explain things by coming up with ideas about the way things work. These scientific ideas are known as hypotheses. When scientists believe they have collected **evidence** that shows their idea is correct, the idea becomes a **theory**.

How Ideas Change

Scientists test ideas to see if they are right or wrong. They put together many conclusions and facts produced by these tests to help prove their scientific ideas. Scientists test new ideas all the time, but their ideas are built on the theories of scientists who came before them. Some of history's greatest scientists completely changed the way people thought about the world.

Scientists use scientific equipment, such as microscopes, to find out more about nature and the world around them.

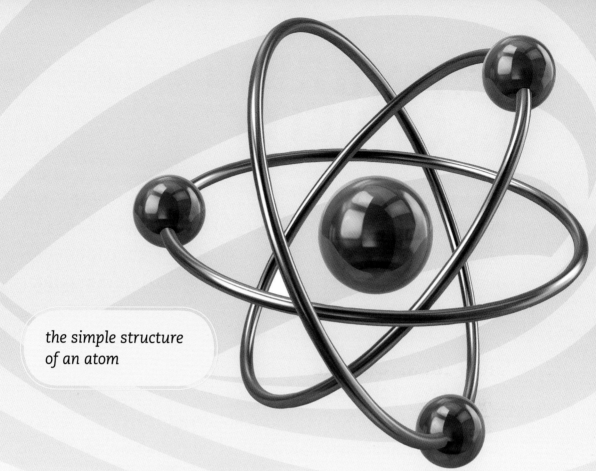

the simple structure of an atom

Universal Building Blocks

Some scientific theories take a long time to prove. In 400 BC, in ancient Greece, a man called Democritus (460–370 BC) had an idea. He found that sand grains could be halved, halved again, and so on, but eventually they couldn't be cut any smaller. Democritus called the tiniest pieces that remained **atoms**. He wondered if everything was made of atoms. It was not until about 2,000 years later that technology, such as powerful microscopes, allowed scientists to test and prove his idea, so it became a theory.

Electricity

Today we know that atoms are the building blocks of everything in the universe. We also know that atoms are made up of smaller particles, including **electrons**. Electricity happens when electrons escape from an atom and flow through a material. The story of the theory of electricity wouldn't be complete without the contribution of many different scientists.

DISCOVERING ELECTRICITY

Electricity is incredibly important. It is the form of energy that lights up our homes, streets, and cities. Electricity makes machines such as TVs, smartphones, and trains work. Everything we know and understand about electricity today is the result of scientific ideas, discoveries, and experiments.

Feather Trick

One day, in around 600 BC, a man known as Thales of Miletus (624–545 BC) was cleaning a chunk of amber with a silk cloth. Amber is a precious orange material made from hardened tree resin. Thales observed that feathers stuck to the amber. He was convinced that this was the work of the gods. We know now it was the work of electrons.

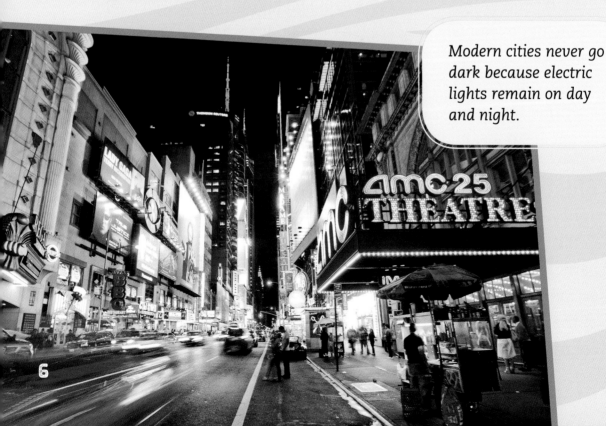

Modern cities never go dark because electric lights remain on day and night.

AMBER=ELEKTRON

Thales did not use the word "electricity." It was invented in 1600 by William Gilbert (1544–1603). Gilbert celebrated Thales' discovery by basing the word on *elektron*. This is the ancient Greek word for amber.

What Happened?

Electrons move around the outside of atoms and have a **negative charge**. The center of an atom, called the nucleus, has a **positive charge**. Electrons usually stay around atoms because they are pulled toward this positive charge. Rubbing the amber removed some electrons from its atoms and onto the silk. This removed the negative charge from the amber atoms, so they had a positive charge. Electrons in the feather atoms were then pulled towards the amber, making the feathers stick to it. Thales had discovered **static electricity**. This is a type of energy resulting from something having too many or too few electrons.

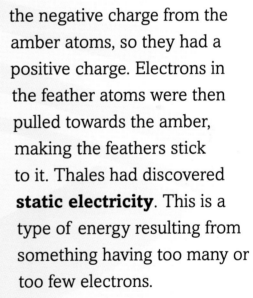

Rubbing a balloon against your head removes the electrons from the balloon and adds them to your hair. The hair's negative charge is then attracted to the balloon's positive charge. This makes your hair stand up!

UNDERSTANDING STATIC

In the 1600s and 1700s, people thought static electricity was a spirit, a weird liquid, or a kind of fire. That's because it can cause mysterious movements, noises, and light!

Making Static

Early scientists wanted to study and demonstrate static, but they needed a regular supply. In 1663, Otto von Guericke (1602–1686) in Germany invented the first static **generator**. By turning a handle, his machine spun a ball on an axle. The ball developed a positive charge when rubbed against a cloth. In 1705, the English scientist Francis Hauksbee (1660–1713) used a generator to produce bright light from a spinning glass globe. This was astonishing because in those days the only sources of light were the sun, fires, lamps, and candles.

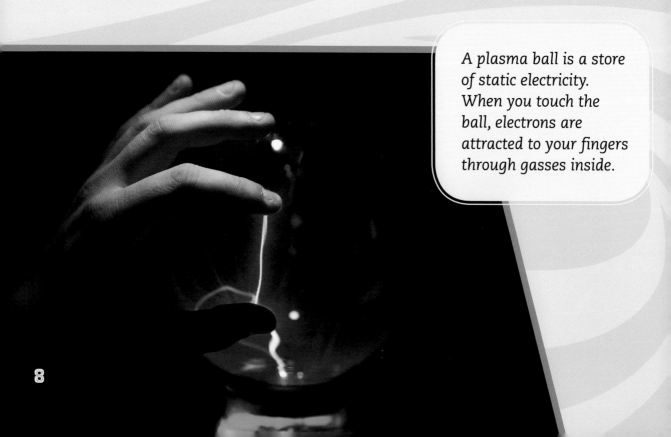

A plasma ball is a store of static electricity. When you touch the ball, electrons are attracted to your fingers through gasses inside.

Trapping Static

In 1745, German scientist Ewald Georg von Kleist (1700–1748) accidentally touched his static generator with a metal nail stuck through a cork into a jar. Later he touched the nail and felt a jolt through his body. We now know that this was an electric shock caused by electricity flowing from the jar into his body. Electrons had moved along the nail and built up in the jar. His accidental invention is known as a Leyden jar.

NAMING THE JAR

The Leyden jar got its name from a town in the Netherlands. This was where, in 1746, a Dutch scientist, Pieter van Musschenbroek (1692–1761), invented a static jar like von Kleist's. As news spread, people named the jar after the place where it was made. Few people heard about von Kleist's earlier invention until years later, but by then, the Leyden jar name had stuck.

a copy of van Musschenbroek's Leyden jar

Electric Clouds

The most exciting effects from Leyden jars were sparks. They could jump from a metal pole on top of the jar to a nearby object. In the early 1700s, people started to notice the similarities between these sparks in laboratories and lightning. They wondered if both were caused by electricity. By then, people knew some of the basics of electricity, such as how it flows through some materials and can make sparks.

Franklin's Theory

Benjamin Franklin (1706–1790) was a famous American scientist. In 1750, he came up with a theory that lightning happened because clouds had an electrical charge. He wanted to test this theory by holding a tall iron rod to draw electricity from the cloud through his body. This rather dangerous experiment would cause a spark to leap from his free hand to a wire connected to the ground.

Scientists now know that lightning is caused by static electricity in clouds.

Testing the Theory

Because other scientists said it was pointless, Franklin did not do his experiment. However, two years later, Frenchman Thomas Dalibard (1703–1799) successfully tested Franklin's theory. He was lucky not to be harmed by the dangerously powerful electrical charges in the cloud.

Breakthrough Moment

SPARKS FLY!

Franklin thought of a better test for his theory in 1752. He used a kite in place of the iron rod, because it could get closer to the cloud. Franklin flew the kite in a storm and tied a metal key to the wet kite string. Franklin saw a spark jump from the key to his body, proving that thunderstorms contain electricity.

Further Investigations

In the early 1700s, people thought that sparks flew because two different electrical fluids moved around. Through testing, Franklin realized that there were positive charges and negative charges, not two fluids. Sparks flew when electrons jumped from a place with a negative charge to one with a positive charge. This canceled out or balanced the charges in either place. His study of electricity in the **atmosphere** proved that electricity is not just a fun trick. It is an important part of the world around us.

BENJAMIN FRANKLIN

Franklin made his fortune as a printer and newspaper editor. In his forties, Franklin studied science and invented many devices, including the lightning rod. This is a metal spike that protects buildings from lightning strikes. Franklin also set up libraries, postal services and a university. He even found time to be a famous politician!

The Next Steps

It is not since the late1800s that scientists have learned more about atmospheric electricity. Then new technology became available, such as cameras to take pictures of lightning. This revealed that sparks have different shapes, which form in different cloud types. Scientists used other technology to measure the size of the electrical **currents** from storm clouds. They discovered that different parts of clouds have different charges. They also found that ice crystals in thunderclouds develop electrical charges when they crash together.

Ice crystals in thunderclouds cause electrical charges, shown in red. They meet with the positive charges coming from the highest point on the ground. In this case, the tree and the bush on the hill are what the lightning strikes.

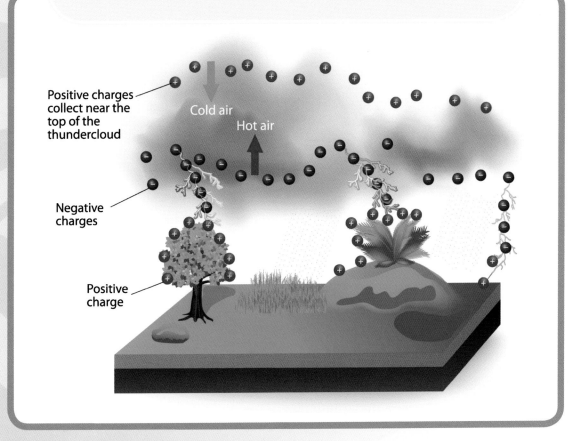

Positive charges collect near the top of the thundercloud

Cold air

Hot air

Negative charges

Positive charge

STORING POWER

When a TV remote stops working, you replace the batteries. You recharge the battery in a cell phone by plugging it into a power source. Batteries are useful stores of power, but the story of batteries only began in the late 1700s.

Static Problems

In those days, scientists used Leyden jars as power sources for experiments. But static electricity only occurs once. Electrons only keep flowing long enough to balance positive and negative charges in materials. Scientists constantly needed to recharge Leyden jars with static generators. To be able to make batteries, they would need a current of electricity.

Batteries are handy stores of chemicals that release power in a device.

Mystery of the Twitching Leg

In the 1780s, a scientist called Luigi Galvani (1737–1798) was studying electrical forces in animals at an Italian university. He had pinned a dead frog's legs to his workbench using brass hooks. Galvani connected a wire from a static generator to one of the frog's legs and saw it twitch as if it were alive. But then he saw the same twitch when the power was not connected as he cut into the legs with a steel knife. Galvani's theory was that animals contain a source of electrical fluid that he called animal electricity. It was this that made the legs twitch.

Breakthrough Moment

FISHY SPARKS

In the 1700s, people knew that touching fish such as torpedo rays caused pain, but they did not believe it was an electric shock. Amateur scientist John Walsh (1726–1795) showed it was electricity by demonstrating a visible spark from the fish in 1776. It was through Walsh's work that Galvani became interested in the effects of electricity in frogs and other animals.

Torpedo rays use their shocking ability to stun prey and also to defend themselves.

Batteries

Alessandro Volta (1745–1827) disagreed with Galvani's theory of animal electricity. Volta believed the leg twitch was caused by electricity flowing through it. He set out to find out why and ended up inventing the first battery in history!

Electricity from Metal

Volta repeated Galvani's experiments and realized that the electrical current did not come from within the frog. In fact, it was made by the metals of the knife and hooks used to pin down the legs. Volta called it metallic electricity. He then tested different combinations of metals to see if he could produce bigger currents. In one experiment, he touched different metals on his tongue. The spit in his mouth conducted electricity, so it tasted bitter.

Alessandro Volta

A Stack of Discs

Volta then wanted to prove that a current could be generated without the need for any animal parts. In 1800, he built a stack of silver and zinc discs. Each was separated from the next one by cloth soaked in saltwater. The arrangement was based on the muscles that make shocks in torpedo rays. He attached a wire to each end and a steady electric current flowed. This stack of discs was the first battery.

BETTER BATTERIES

Volta generated a bigger **voltage**, or push of current, by adding more discs or by using different metals. Over the next 100 years, scientists developed better batteries. For example, they replaced saltwater with **acid** and wet chemicals with dry chemicals. These made batteries smaller, more powerful, and longer lasting. The drone is one of many machines that has been made possible by the development of better, longer-lasting batteries as a source of power.

ELECTRICITY AND MAGNETS

In the 1800s, many scientists began to look for connections between electricity and **magnetism**, which can both make things move. In 1820, a Danish scientist called Hans Christian Oersted (1777–1851) put his magnetic compass down on a workbench. It happened to be near a wire connected to a battery. Oersted spotted the compass needle twitching when he turned on the battery and an electric current passed through the wire. This proved electricity and magnetism are connected.

Oersted, demonstrating the connection between electricity and magnetism to other scientists.

RELATED FORCES

In 1820, French mathematician Andre-Marie Ampère (1775–1836) developed a theory that the sizes of electrical and magnetic forces are related. He found that two wires with a current going through them were either pulled together or pushed apart depending on the direction of the current. Later, the unit to measure the size of a current was named Ampère, or Amp.

Electromagnetism

Other scientists tried to make magnets using electrical currents through wires. In 1820, François Arago (1786–1853) demonstrated how iron filings lined up around a **coil** of copper wire when a current went through it. Then, in 1825, the British scientist William Sturgeon (1783–1850) built the first **electromagnet** for a scientific demonstration. He coiled wire cable around an iron bar 18 times. It could pick up 20 times its own weight when the power was on, but it was just an iron bar when there was no current. Four years later, the American Joseph Henry (1797–1878) improved on the design. By coiling more wire around a metal bar, he created an electromagnet that could lift more than a ton!

Maglev trains use powerful electromagnets to lift them above guide rails.

Currents Using Magnets

Now scientists knew that currents could make magnets. In 1831, Michael Faraday (1791–1867), a British scientist, figured out how to use magnets to create electricity.

Faraday's original coil. His invention transformed how we produce electricity.

Moving Magnets

Several scientists had noticed a weak current flowing through a coil of wire when they put a magnet inside. A magnet has an area around it where there is a magnetic force. It is called the magnetic field. Most magnets have two ends where the magnetic field has different effects. One end pulls magnetic objects towards it and the other pushes them away.

Faraday's Theory

Faraday wondered whether changing the magnetic field around a magnet could create a current in an unconnected wire. He tested this by switching an electromagnet on and off. Faraday saw that a current flowed first one way and then the other. He found that stronger electromagnets and bigger changes in the magnetic field produced bigger currents. Then Faraday tried moving a magnet in and out of a coil of wire. He created a steady current. This was the first generator.

Generators

Most electric power we use today is made with generators based on this idea. In most generators, spinning magnets or spinning wire coils are used to produce currents. The spinning movement is usually produced by the push of wind, water, or steam on the blades of turbines. Turbines are machines that change a push from one direction into a spinning motion. Turbines in power stations produce most of the world's electricity.

A *generator is inside the box behind the blade of each wind turbine. It converts energy from moving air into electricity.*

MOVING ELECTRICITY

During the late 1800s, demand for electricity increased as electric lights spread to homes, factories, and streets. Electric lights meant people could stay up later, work longer, and see better as they walked home at night. People already used gas lamps in homes and streets, which produced light by burning gas. However, gas could cause fires, and the light from the lamps was weaker than from electric bulbs. The problem was where to get the power from.

In the 1800s, electricity was a novelty because it was still in short supply.

Power Sources

Street lights and machines, such as streetcars, often used battery power. But the batteries stored very little power and often ran down. Factories and homes with electric lights needed their own generators, but they were usually noisy, dirty, very expensive machines. These generators needed a lot of coal to work.

Power for All

In 1882, inventor and businessman Thomas Edison (1847–1931) changed that. He built the world's first **power plant** in New York City. A power plant is a factory that produces electricity. Cables carried electricity from the large generator in the plant to homes and businesses nearby. Gradually, small power stations based on Edison's designs were built in cities across the US.

CHANGING STATIONS

An average power station makes power for about 1 million people. Today, New York City is much bigger than in Edison's day and has a population of over 8.5 million people. So it relies on many power stations to meet its demand for electricity.

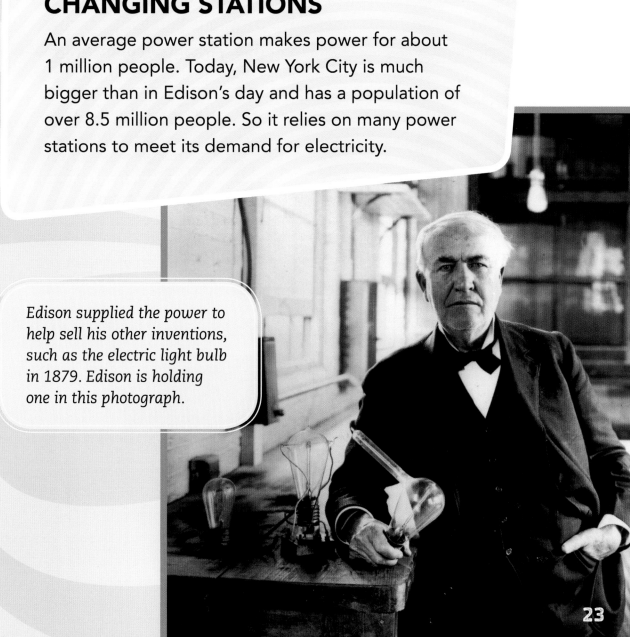

Edison supplied the power to help sell his other inventions, such as the electric light bulb in 1879. Edison is holding one in this photograph.

Types of Currents

A generator produces **alternating current** (**AC**). The current changes direction often as the coil passes different magnetic fields. Edison designed his power station to produce **direct current** (**DC**). His DC supply was made by fitting a machine to an AC generator that changed the current.

Energy Loss

The problem with DC electricity is that some of the electrical energy changes into heat as it moves long distances through wires. In the late 1880s, Edison hired a young Serbian scientist named Nikola Tesla (1856–1943). Tesla did improve Edison's DC system, but he believed that AC was the future of electricity supply.

Electric motors make all kinds of things work, from smoothie makers to drills and TVs. They are all based on Tesla's designs, such as this small AC motor from around 1888.

Tesla and AC Power

Tesla left Edison and set up his own company to develop AC electricity. Tesla had a theory that AC power could be sent over long distances if its voltage was increased. He designed machines called **transformers** to do this, plus high-voltage power cables, lights, and **electric motors**. But Tesla could not afford to actually build the system. A rich businessman, George Westinghouse (1846–1914), heard about Tesla's inventions. He paid for Tesla's ideas and built the AC system. It worked! Thomas Edison was unhappy about this, so he spread the word that AC was dangerous. He even paid for stray dogs to be electrocuted by AC power at public events as a warning!

Nikola Tesla

Breakthrough Moment

CHICAGO WORLD'S FAIR

In 1893, crowds were astonished when over 200,000 lights went on at the Colombian Exposition at the Chicago World's Fair. The organizers had chosen AC power rather than DC. Today, almost all power we use is supplied as AC systems based on Tesla's work.

Power Options

The world's growing population needs more and more power each year. The problem is how to produce power without harming our planet.

Changing Power

Most electricity comes from power stations that run on coal and gas. These are fossil fuels, which means they formed from the remains of living things that died millions of years ago. Burning these fuels releases harmful gases into Earth's atmosphere. They trap heat in a process called global warming. This is causing an increase in our planet's average temperature. In turn, this is affecting weather patterns, so there are more fierce storms, for example. This is why countries are trying to make more power using wind, water, and waves. These **green energy** sources have no fuel costs and will not run out, unlike fossil fuels.

Fossil fuels are used to fuel power stations like this one.

There are now many solar farms around the world with solar panels producing power from solar energy.

New Generation

In 1954, a team of U.S. scientists created the first **solar cells**. These devices contain thin slices of special materials that produce a current when sunlight hits them. Solar cells were developed to supply power to spacecraft far from Earth's electricity supply. They are still used in space today, but also on Earth. Today, solar cells can be found on many things, such as watches and street lights. Panels of many cells connected together create larger amounts of power.

USING LESS POWER

In addition to using more green energy, many people are trying to cut their power use. They do this by turning off machines when they are not in use. People also choose to buy machines, such as TVs and refrigerators, that are more energy efficient. This means they use less power than other machines to do the same job.

QUIZ

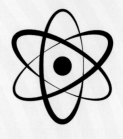

1. What is the smallest particle in an atom?

2. What does a Leyden jar store?

3. Who flew a kite in a storm to prove that storm clouds are electric?

4. On which animal did Luigi Galvani do his experiment?

5. Who invented the first battery, or pile, in Italy in 1800?

6. What is produced around a wire when a current flows through it?

7. What kind of magnet only works when it is switched on?

8. Who invented the first generator that produced a current of electricity?

9. How many types of currents are there?

10. Which device turns light energy into electrical energy?

For the answers to this quiz, see page 31

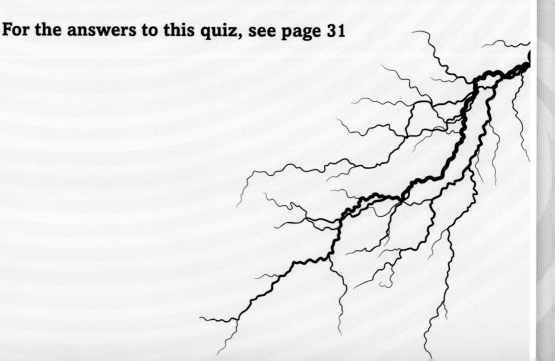

TIMELINE

600 BC Thales of Miletus sees static electricity between amber and feathers

400 BC Democritus says that everything is made of atoms

AD 1600 William Gilbert first uses the word "electricity"

1663 Otto von Guericke invents the first static generator

1705 Francis Hauksbee uses a generator to produce light

1745 Ewald Georg von Kleist accidentally invents a store of static electricity in a jar

1746 Pieter van Musschenbroek invents the Leyden jar

1750 Benjamin Franklin suggests that lightning happens because clouds have an electric charge; this idea is tested by Thomas Dalibard

1752 Franklin proves his 1750 theory

1776 John Walsh demonstrates a spark from an electric fish

1780s Luigi Galvani shows electricity can make the legs of a dead frog twitch

1800 Alessandro Volta invents the first battery

1820 Hans Christian Oersted discovers that electrical currents produce a magnetic field

1820 Andre-Marie Ampère suggests a link between the size of a current and the size of magnetic fields

1825 William Sturgeon demonstrates the first electromagnet

1829 Joseph Henry builds the first practical electromagnet

1831 Michael Faraday invents the generator

1879 Thomas Edison invents the first practical light bulb

1882 Edison builds the first direct current (DC) power plant

1886–87 Nikola Tesla invents his alternating current (AC) electrical supply system

1954 Daryl Chapin, Calvin Fuller, and Gerald Pearson invent the first solar cell

GLOSSARY

acid—a strong substance that often tastes sour and attracts electrons

alternating current (AC)—a current that changes direction very quickly

atmosphere—the layer of gasses surrounding a planet

atom—the smallest building block of everything in the Universe

coil—to wind a length of something, such as a rope or wire, around something else

current—the flow of electrons through an object

direct current (DC)—a current that flows in only one direction

electric motor—a device in which an electromagnet and a permanent magnet repel each other to produce movement

electromagnet—a device that becomes a magnet when a current flows through it

electron—the smallest particle within an atom; electrons move around its center

evidence—a collection of information or facts that prove if something is true or not

generator—a machine that makes electricity using movement of magnets next to coils of wire

green energy—energy sources such as wind and water that are free, will not run out and that have little harmful impact on the atmosphere

magnetism—the power to attract or repel in materials, caused by movement of electric charge

negative charge—when something has too many electrons

positive charge—when something has too few electrons

power plant—a factory that makes electricity to send elsewhere, often by burning fossil fuels

solar cell—a device that makes a direct current of power when sunlight shines on layers of special materials

static electricity—the type of energy resulting from something having too many or too few electrons

theory—a scientific idea with evidence to back it up

transformer—a machine that can increase or decrease the voltage of an electrical current

voltage—the force of an electrical current; voltage is measured in volts

READ MORE

BOOKS

Amson-Bradshaw, Georgia. *Electricity* (Science in a Flash). London, U.K.:Franklin Watts, 2017.

Claybourne, Anna. *Electricity and Magnets* (Mind Webs). London, U.K.: Wayland, 2016.

Graham, Ian. *From Falling Water to Electric Car* (Energy Journeys). North Mankato, Minn.: Heinemann, 2015.

Oxlade, Chris. *Electricity* (How Does My Home Work?). North Mankato, Minn.: Heinemann-Raintree, 2012.

INTERNET SITES

Use Facthound to find Internet sites related to this book.

Visit *www.facthound.com*

Just type in 9781410987273 and go!

Check out projects, games and lots more at
www.capstonekids.com

ANSWERS TO QUIZ

1. Electron; **2.** Static electricity; **3.** Benjamin Franklin; **4.** A frog; **5.** Alessandro Volta; **6.** Magnetic field; **7.** Electromagnet; **8.** Michael Faraday; **9.** Two: alternating (AC) and direct (DC); **10.** A solar cell

INDEX